# Seahorses

By Jenna Lee Gleisner

SPARKS

# Picture Glossary

seahorse 8

seaweed 6

**stingray**     **14**

**sunfish**     **10**

This is an angelfish.

An angelfish lives in the sea.

angelfish

This is seaweed.

Seaweed grows in the sea.

seaweed

This is a seahorse.

A seahorse lives in the sea.

seahorse

This is a sunfish.

A sunfish lives in the sea.

sunfish

This is a starfish.

A starfish lives in the sea.

starfish

13

This is a stingray.

A stingray lives in the sea.

stingray

# Do You Know?

## What animal is this?

angelfish

seahorse

sunfish

starfish